DON'T BE A FOOL GO TO SCHOOL

Why College is for You

by Derek Chatman

Table of Contents

ABOUT THE AUTHOR

Derek S. Chatman was born in Springfield, Massachusetts, the home of Dr. Seuss and the Basketball Hall of Fame. While working as a Security Guard for a major paper manufacturer, he dreamed of one day leaving his dead end security job and having an actual office in the building he was protecting. While working security Derek would return to school and pursue his passion of obtaining a Bachelor's Degree and a job in corporate America. Believing that any and everything in life is attainable if you stay focused and believe in yourself and your abilities. Derek would earn a Bachelor's Degree in Business Management from American International College. His passion didn't stop there; he would continue the education momentum and obtained an MBA from his alma mater. Derek used his degrees and his business knowledge to successfully climb the corporate ladder and currently has an office in the exact location that he dreamed of years before.

"Live as if you were to die tomorrow. Learn as if you were to live forever."

— Mahatma Gandhi

"You educate a man; you educate a man. You educate a woman; you educate a generation."

— Brigham Young

"When you know better you do better."

— Maya Angelou

"Intelligence plus character-that is the goal of true education."

— Martin Luther King Jr.

"The journey of a thousand miles starts with a single step."
- **Chinese Proverb**

CHAPTER 1
WHY COLLEGE IS FOR ME

If you are reading this book then you have probably come to a point in your life where you feel a college education could be beneficial in improving the quality of your life.

Well you have come to the right place!

You may want to get an education to land a better job, a job that will pay you more than what you are currently making today. You may be interested in totally changing your field of work or you may feel you are stuck in your current position and want to use an education to help you climb up the corporate ladder. You may want to increase your knowledge in a certain field for your own personal growth or you may be just plain fed up with your current job and want an education to become the means to help get you out of the madness! All of these reasons are valid and an education can truly be the remedy. This book is designed to help those who have questions, concerns, doubts or are a little hesitant to take the plunge into the world of higher education. Let me tell you right now a college education is 100% achievable no matter what the circumstances are in your life right now. If you follow the methods outlined in this book, you will achieve this. Now you're probably

saying to yourself: *"Year right, he has no idea what he's talking about. I have my own valid set of reasons on why I can't go to school right now. I will eventually go to school when the time is right."* Well guess what if you keep that mentality the time will never ever be right for you. It's like saying "I want to drive to the movies, but the only way I will go is if all of the traffic lights from my home to the movie theater are green. I don't want a red light to hinder my progress." As ridiculous as that sounds, that is exactly what a person sounds like when they are waiting for the "perfect time" and situation to go to school. The perfect scenario will never present itself. You have to just get in your car and drive. You will get there. You may have to stop at a few red lights, or make your way through a little bit of traffic, but in the end you will find your way to your goal.

"That is easy for you to say Derek I bet you went to college right out of high school and your parents paid for you to go to some fancy Ivy League school, and I bet you had no other obligations to focus on except for your education." My college experience was quite the contrary. Even though I did start my college education right out of high school, I didn't complete it until I was well into my thirties. At the time I graduated from college I was a father of two, a husband, and I was in a comfortable yet dead in job where I worked rotating shifts and

12 hours on the weekends at a minimum of fifty six work hours a week. I was able to do it, juggle life and school, and I would be a complete liar if I were to tell you it wasn't a challenge, because indeed it was. However it was a challenge that was manageable and I did not miss out on any of the finer things in life, like spending time with my family or going on vacation, and I still found the time to enjoy friends and all of my hobbies. I simply prioritized, made the decision and jumped into my education full steam ahead.

In this book I will show you the methods I used to achieve it along with stories of people who are similar to you who found a way to get an education and graduate from college and improve their lives.

It is natural in our society to believe we have no time to pursue our passions. We are in a constant race against a self-imposed clock. Where do I find the time and the motivation to do it? There is time for everything and if you believe your scenario is unique and you have no way to get this done. I am here to tell you that there is a way.

Listed below are the reasons why we feel we can't go to school right now. I can't list them all because it would probably fill this entire book. Instead I will list the top 5.

TOP 5 EXCUSES

WHY COLLEGE IS NOT FOR ME RIGHT NOW

1. **I DON'T HAVE THE TIME**

2. **I CAN'T AFFORD IT**

3. **I HAVE NEEDS TO TEND TO**

4. **I HAVE NO ONE TO WATCH MY CHILDREN**

5. **I AM NOT SMART ENOUGH**

This list is filled with exactly what the heading describes, EXCUSES. If we want to we can think of an excuse to justify just about anything in life. We have to stop making excuses and get up and make life better. When we are ready we have to simply register for our first class and go. Sounds quite simple and truly it is simple. It's fear in our head that holds us back.

CHAPTER 2
I DON'T HAVE THE TIME

Kevin Zimmerman a great family friend of mine has an autobiography written about his life titled "A TIME FOR EVERYTHING, THE KEVIN ZIMMERMAN STORY". This is one of life's truest statements. There is indeed a time for everything we want in our lives. We have to merely prioritize and make space for personal and spiritual growth along with making space for the things we love. Get out there and enjoy life. We owe it to ourselves. Often we get caught up in our daily routine and we feel like we are on a never ending treadmill

Wake up in the morning- walk the dog-off to work -rush home-take the kids to soccer practice- cook dinner-make sure the children finish their homework-off to bed-wake up and repeat this cycle year after year. The specific components of your daily routine may be slightly different, but the outcome is exactly the same. It's truly life's treadmill; we are doing all of this walking, however in the end we never really went anywhere. We take no time to grow.

If you have to plant seeds and you dreamed of one day planting them in your backyard and watching them bloom into a beautiful

garden. If you stop and think about it, you have all of the necessary components to make this successful, right at your fingertips. You have an endless supply of sun, water, soil and most importantly seed. Now all that is left to turn this into a beautiful garden is your time and effort. You go to the store and purchase a variety of seed packets and you envision what your garden is going to look like once it has bloomed. You get home and you place the seed packets on the kitchen counter and say to yourself "Tomorrow I am going to get out there and plant them. I don't have time right now, but when I do have time I am going to cultivate a garden." You have the greatest intentions in the world, but successes worst enemy PROCRASTINATION is lurking around corner planting excuses in your mind. You see the seed packets on the counter every morning at breakfast and every evening at dinnertime, and each day you promise yourself when your busy schedule slows down a bit you are going to start your garden. Well the days turn into weeks, and the weeks turn into months, and the months turn into years and you never found the time to start your garden. That is because you did not make it a priority. When you prioritize and set time aside for yourself, the time to get it done will present itself. The seeds are not going to miraculously jump off the kitchen counter and plant themselves. They need you to take a little time to plant them in the ground, cultivate the soil, water them and make sure they have access to the sun. With minimal effort they will grow all by themselves. That is what it takes to pursue a college education. Plant your seed of knowledge for yourself and take a little time and give it all the necessities it needs to grow and before your know it, your life will be in full bloom.

Often times as an adult we realize our lives have taken on a multitude of responsibilities. The responsibilities eventually consume all of our time.

Please take a moment, sit down in a quiet place and clear your mind of everything. Truly stop, reflect and think about these questions.

What am I doing for myself?

What am I doing to help myself grow and evolve into a better person?

Am I being the best that I can be?

Am I maximizing my full potential?

Do I have three hours in my week to take a class?

Most of the time we may think we are doing things for ourselves, but when we scratch the surface we will discover we are truly not

doing enough. Most of the time we are helping others which is a noble within itself, or we are simply doing the things to maintain the level of the life we are currently living. Now imagine if you reached your full potential, how much more you could help others and live a more fruitful life.

Our responsibilities in life can vary. You can be a mother with young children and a full time job or you can be single parent with a full time job and an elderly parent who needs your care several times a week. You may be a father who works the nightshift in a factory who spends his days sleeping in between getting his children off to school and home from school every day. When you look at all of these scenarios you will see they all have one thing in common. Each person is living in their comfort zone or a stagnant part of their lives. On the outside it may look good, but being comfortable can sometimes be your worst enemy. You may own a home, have a nice car, have all of your bills paid, but are you truly pursuing your life's dream? Are you doing a job just to pay the bills? Do you go through your life tired? Do you dread Monday mornings? Our goal in life should be to pursue our passions. When we are doing the things we love. It's no longer a chore. Getting an education and training that will lead you down the path of your passion is the first step.

Now raising your children or helping a sick parent or trying to advance in your career are all life defining goals, but if you are not happy and are not pursuing your passions your efforts will not be your best. You are not being the best person you know you can be. If going to school getting an education or getting the training so you

can pursue a career path that you are passionate about will improve your life dramatically.

Let's say you work a job that you do not particularly care about in a field that you don't really care about. In essence it is not even close to being your dream job. Your manager has been on you all day trying to pressure you into increasing your productivity and meet a dead line. The culture, the rules and the environment of the job are just too restricting for you. It feels like the business controls every aspect of your life, leaving no room for creativity and growth. It feels like you are doing more work than your co-workers with half of the recognition and none of the job advancement they are receiving because they are the manager's personal pet. The work day leaves you frustrated and tired. You get home and you are mentally and physically exhausted. Now it's time for family. It seems your children have more energy than ever; they are bouncing off of the walls with excitement. All you want to do is take a hot bath and go to bed, but you love your family and you want to spend quality time with them. Your children's brotherly wrestling match and the brotherly screams coming from the family room are like needles poking at your brain. You run into the room and you scream "knock it off now!" Your protest immediately kills the

enthusiasm in the room. All of the loving and positive energy just went out of the window. Your family just absorbed all of your negative energy. Because of your scream session dinner is quiet, the kids and your spouse walk on egg shells around you because they know you had a tough unfulfilled day at work and if they knew what was best for them they would continue their night avoiding you for fear of irritating the frustrated beast that took over their parent's mind and body. Now on the outside it appears you spent your evening constructively at home with family, but if you were truly happy with your life. The time spent would have been of better quality.

Let's say your passions are to work for a company like the American Red Cross where you spend most of your time helping others. The job totally feels like the place you want to be, it maximizes all of the skills that come easy and natural to you. You spend all of your day at an outdoor drive assisting people who are donating blood for the hospitals in need. The day is long and hot, you must have assisted at least 100 willing donators. At the end of the day you are exhausted, but you feel great. You feel a great sense of accomplishment. The day went by quick and as a matter of a fact it didn't even feel like work because you were doing what you love to do. You leave work with a sense of pride and accomplishment because you made a difference in the world today. The world is a better place because of you. On the drive home you dream about

soaking in the bathtub, and how it will revitalize your muscles from a busy day. You walk through the front door of the house and your two children and your spouse are in the middle of a full-fledged squirt gun battle. Now you have warned them millions of times about using the water pistols in the house and wetting up the floors and your precious furniture. Now if you were coming home from a long frustrating day at job you hated. Your first reaction would have been to go in the house and yell at absolutely everyone for violating your no squirt guns in the house policy. However, today you are not frustrated, you are tired but not frustrated because you had a great day doing something you love, so your mentality is totally different. The family had not seen you yet, so you sneak up to the bedroom, go into the closet and grab the gigantic super soaker water gun you hid from the family. You fill it up with what seems like gallons of water and you run down and attack your unsuspecting family, winning the water gun battle single handedly. Your positive energy brings the family to a whole new level. You spend the rest of the night laughing and joking with the family as you describe your great day at work and they describe their great summer day at home.

In both scenarios you come from home from a long day of work exhausted, but the scenario and the quality of family time improved once you were doing something you love?

Go to school pursue your passion! Live life the way you want it to be!

There are so many programs out there that cater to a busy lifestyle. You can go to school at night, on the weekends; you can take online courses, blended courses that are taught in a classroom and virtually. There is no excuse. We can all spare three hours out of the 168 hours we have in a week. That is less than 2% of your time a week to help change your life. The time to achieve your dreams in now and it starts with the first step. Register for your first class.

CHAPTER 3
I CANT AFFORD IT

There is a myth that only financially well off people can afford to go to college. This is completely untrue. Every single person on this planet can go to college. It's just a matter of saying you are going to do it and going out and doing it. This may sound simple, but it's completely true. There are so many financial options available out there to help you pay for college. You have to find the right avenue that suits you and your situation best. Sometimes it may take multiple avenues to help pay tuition, but don't let the lack of funds stop you from pursuing your dreams.

A good place to start is with Federal financial aid. The federal government offer's over 150 million dollars in the form of loans, grants and work study funds, this money can be used to pay for tuition as well as room and board at whatever place of higher education across the United States you choose. What's great is the government financing is not exclusive to traditional colleges and universities. It can also be used to finance career schools, graduate schools and professional schools. Visit the website Studentloans.gov for more information. To get started simply fill out the Free Application for Federal Student Aid (FAFSA).

Does this sound a bit intimidating? It's not. The application is free and it can be filled out online at Studentloans.gov, and will only take you 30 minutes to complete.

Federal Student Aid an office of the U.S Department of Education defines Grants, Loans and Work study as:

Grants –financial aid that doesn't have to be repaid (unless, for example you withdraw from school and owe a refund)

Loans –borrowed money for college or career school you must repay with interest

Work Study –a work program through which you can earn money to help pay for school.

Federal funds are not the only avenue to receive financing; you can also look at your own local city and state for financial aid. Visit the website ED.gov for more information on scholarships, grants and state programs that offer assistance.

Another avenue for financial aid that is very similar to the programs offered by the federal government is aid from private or nonprofit organizations.

Private institutions like banks and credit unions offer financing that can be used for direct and indirect education related expenses.

Loans can cover education costs, including all of the things you will need while pursuing an education, like books, housing and computers. The benefits will vary based upon the financial institution that provides the loan, however most institutions will not request installed payments until after finishing school on the loans they offer at fixed or variable interest rates.

SCHOLARSHIPS are another finance option you should most definitely pursue. You would be knocked off of your feet when you discover the number of institutions that offer scholarships that can cover a part or even the cost of your entire education. Scholarships are offered based upon a variety of things that may relate to you and your situation. It could be academics, athletics, career field, cultural ethnicity, hobbies – the list could go on for days. You name it and a scholarship may be attached to it. Major corporations, churches, clubs, foundations and community organizations all offer free scholarships. Visit the local office of an organization that may relate to you or visit their website for more information.

The financing avenue I pursued when I returned to college to receive my Bachelors and Master Degree in business was through a tuition reimbursement program offered at my place of employment.

My job like many large number of business offered 100% payment of my school tuition in a field that related to the business based upon the grade I received for each class.

For example if I received the following grades, my company would pay the following percentage:

A = 100% tuition paid

B= 100% tuition paid

C= 100% tuition paid

D=75% tuition paid

An educated employee is a benefit to both the employee and employer. Employees tend to be more productive, more educated, along with increasing their tenor with the employer who is paying their tuition. Tuition reimbursement programs are now being bundled along with a company's other benefits like health insurance, 401K and vacation time as a marketing tool to attract prospective employees. Some companies may require the employee to stay with the company for a certain time period and some employers may not have any requirement at all. Please check with your companies Human Resource department for more information. You may be presently surprised that the company you work for offers this benefit.

UNCLE SAM also has programs that pay for college tuition through there GI bill as well as other programs. These programs are offered to active and inactive duty members as well as reservists in several branches of the military. The coverage can include graduate, undergraduate degrees, and training programs. Please visit a local military office in your area or visit the United States Department of Veteran Affairs website www.gibill.va.gov for more information.

Finally, if you can't beat them join them. Some Colleges and Universities offer free tuition or partial paid tuition to employees who work full time and or part time for their institution.

This benefit depends upon the individual policies of the place of higher education. This may be a benefit worth pursuing to cover some of or all of your tuition. Also as a side benefit, some of the colleges or university may extend the paid tuition to your family members as well. Please check with your selected place of higher education for more details.

CHAPTER 4
I HAVE NEEDS TO TEND TO

The time will never ever be perfect to start pursuing an education. As we get deeper into our lives our levels of responsibility increases. Who said growing up into an adult was easy? When we were children we all dreamed of the day when we would have our own place to live, and the ability to set our own rules, outside of the rules set by our parents. The first few years I was out of my parents' home and living in a condo on my own eating Cap'n Crunch and Fruity Pebbles for dinner became a dinner ritual for me and my fiancé. This would have driven my mother absolutely insane if I was living at home. I could hear her now "cereal is for breakfast, not dinner! Boy put that bowl down!"

Of course this freedom to do whatever you want comes at a price.

In order to afford these freedoms we have to start paying our own bills. Now paying your own bills gives you a greater appreciation of the value of things. At this point you are no longer getting the basic things of life for free. As our needs in life increase, unfortunately so do our bills. This means now we have to make enough money to cover our bills. For a majority of us this means getting a job or starting our own business to earn money. Employment can take up $1/3^{rd}$ of our day if we are lucky, leaving $1/3^{rd}$ for sleeping and the other $1/3^{rd}$ for free time to do whatever we please. In that $1/3^{rd}$ of free time we have during the day it's not actually all "free time" because we have other responsibilities like tending to the needs of our children or we may have family members who need our assistance. We may have pets, hobbies, church, all things that are important to us that leaves us with not much time for anything else. Have you ever noticed when some type of unexpected emergency pops up we all of a sudden find the necessary time to fit it in our daily life? It may come at the expense of something else we had planned that day, but we do indeed make the time. We may have rescheduled an activity, but in the end we find a way to reprioritize. Why don't we do that for an education?

It is an important part of our future.

Let's say you work a day job and during the summer and you get a call from the summer camp nurse saying your daughter just broke her ankle on the playground and they are sending her to the hospital for care. Once you get to the hospital, the doctor informs you your daughter will be fine, however she will need to go to physical therapy twice a week to help the ankle heal and return to normal strength. Now your job doesn't allow you to leave in the middle of the work day, so you get creative and ask to work an extra three hours thought out the rest of the week to make up for the missed time. You are using this time because it is for the welfare and safety of your child, so it is time well spent. We always find ways to be creative when a negative event occurs, but we don't do it for a positive event. Why not use your creativity to help you pursue your dreams? This creativity can turn a dream into a reality, and dramatically change your life for the better.

In the same situation let's say your daughter never broke her ankle and you dream of one day becoming a chef because you love to cook. However the culinary class you like occurs on Tuesday and Thursdays each week for an hour and a half each session for an entire three month semester during the hours you work. Why not ask to be excused for this time and promise to make up the three hours missed another day?

THE REASON WHY I CAN'T:

My job will not allow me to leave in the middle of the day. It is against the company policy.

Sometimes we tell ourselves no before even asking the question. Even if it written in the company's policy it will not hurt to ask, you may be presently surprised at the answer you may receive. Rules are just rules, they can be broken. Even if you do receive a no, get creative and find a way to make it happen.

When I was pursuing my Bachelor's degree in business I worked a rotating shift, with a schedule that was truly unique. The first week of the month I worked first shift, the second week I worked second

shift and the third week of the month I worked third shift. Of course the core business class I wanted to take was only being offered during the daytime and my scheduled made it difficult to attend each week. So I got creative. I pursued every traditional avenue available and no one was willing to help. My co-workers even refused to switch one of their dayshift weeks for my night shift week. So I decided to use half of a vacation day for the three months of day shift to cover the classes. I had to sacrifice vacation time, but it was well worth it and I was still had enough vacation time left to enjoy a week in Disney with my family that year, even though I only had two weeks of vacation time to begin with.

Taken this class was a heaven sent miracle because the class offered a bonus that has paid off for me even to today. This class taught me how to use PowerPoint for presentations and this tool helped me receive a promotion. I taught my then 8 year old daughter how to use it for a class presentation and the teacher and all of the students were so impressed, she was asked to performed the presentation for the entire school. She received an A for the project and the following year, every student's project was in PowerPoint format. It was great way to show my daughter how to be a leader.

The moral of the story is we cannot let our obligations hinder our growth. We all have responsibilities, but we must find ways to make our dreams come true. You can start off slow and take one class on one night a week. Everyone can spare an hour to three

hours a week. It will enrich your life as well as the lives of everyone around us. The needs in life are always going to be there. They will be there before class and they will be there after class. Make the time for yourself. You deserve it. You work hard and you are a great person, reward yourself with personal growth.

CHAPTER 5
I HAVE NO ONE TO WATCH MY CHILDREN

Our children are our pride and joy. It is our job as parents to make sure

they have all of the necessities in life to help them grow into successful

adults. We want to make sure our children reach their full potential and

contribute positively to our society. We want to make sure they have a

roof over their heads, clothing on their backs, food to eat and access to a

quality education. Kids tend to use their parents' lives as models or

guidelines to how they will live their lives. Have you ever noticed how

children grow up and choose similar professions as their parents? Police

officers children become Police officers and Fireman, doctors, nurses, and

teachers children end up following in their parents' footsteps? If you go

to college there is higher likelihood your children will as well. If you don't

attended college there is a high likelihood they will not either. They look

at you and set that as their guideline or marker for life. Why wouldn't you

want to set a positive example? Do you want your children to work in a

field that they do not love or have to go to a job that they absolutely hate,

just so they can make ends meet?

As parents our lives are very busy. We often try to juggle our busy work and family lives. This can often times make us feel a bit guilty for not spending enough time with our children.

The best and most convenient option when you take your first class or classes is to have your spouse or significant other watch the children. When my wife decided to take night and Saturday classes to complete her Bachelor's degree our family dynamic actually got stronger. Once or twice a week when my wife was taking night classes my children and I were on our own to cook dinner and make sure all of the activities like having homework completed, dinner cooked and chores before bedtime completed. It showed my children as well as myself that we can step up and take more responsibility. To be honest we had no choice because my wife was not home to make all of this happen. We definitely gained some appreciation for the job my wife does on a regular basis. My wife was a bit nervous at first, but we stepped up our game and got everything accomplished. It also took a bit of pressure off of her and she felt like she could comfortably step out of her role as mother and wife and just be herself, even if it was for just one or two nights a week.

If your spouse or significant other aren't able to help out with the children while you attend class the next best option would be to choose a family member or friend the kids would absolutely love to

spend time with. Grandparents love to spend time with their grandchildren whenever they can, and the especially love the fact that they can spoil them and then give them back to you.

You could also choose to have the parents of one of your children's classmates watch your child while you are in class. This would give your child someone they can do homework with or perhaps study with as well. This will also give the children something to look forward to during the week. An hour or two a week just for yourself where you can be a bit selfish and enjoy a class of your dreams will work wonders on your self-esteem.

If family and friends are not an option you could look into paying a babysitter for an hour or two during the week. You can always find a responsible teenager or young adult in the neighborhood for a good price. Your money may be a bit tight, but you can always find a little wiggle room in your budget to pay for several hours during the week. When you accomplish your dreams the small price you paid for a sitter will be money well invested.

Ok so now I have someone to watch the children, how am I going to find the time to do my homework?

The answer to this question is be willing to be creative. I used to study during lunch breaks at work or I would purchase audio books and listen to them in the car on the way to work or I would wake up an hour early before work to study. I would make flash cards and study during slow times at work, instead of surfing the internet. You have to be creative; the method will come to you.

As I am writing this book I am on vacation at Disney in Orlando Florida. My wife and my two children and I are sharing a rental home for the week (a very cheap way to enjoy Disney, hopefully I can share this in another book or chapter) with my nephew and his wife and two young children. My nephew and his wife both work full time jobs and they are both HIGHLY active in their children's lives, including soccer practices and games, basketball practice and games, school and regular family outings. My nephew's wife is in a Master's degree program with a full work load of studying and homework. Instead of staying home and not enjoying her life, she brought her laptop on vacation with her. She is sitting by the pool as I type this. She is on her laptop doing homework as her children swim in the pool seven feet away from her. She would spend an hour on the laptop every morning and then put it away and enjoy the pool and the rest of the day with her family. That is the level of creativity you must have to be able to enjoy life and grow along with it. Don't worry about trying to build a giant brick wall. Focus on laying down one brick at a time. Before you know it you will be staring at a wall you built, that will eventually turn into a home.

CHAPTER 6
I AM NOT SMART ENOUGH

For some strange reason the vast majority of people on this earth regardless of race, culture, age, or upbringing underestimate their level of intelligence. We constantly doubt our abilities. Some of the greatest people to ever walk this planet have had their doubts about their capability, but what separates them from the rest of the pack is their unflappable belief in their abilities. They never worry about what the naysayers think, they are not afraid to make mistakes, and more importantly they never doubt their level of intelligence. It is this positive outlook that makes them successful. We all have that little voice in our heads called our conscience that loves to spread doubt in our minds.

"If you go against popular belief everyone else will think you're stupid, and you don't want to look stupid in front of everyone."

How many times have you sat in classroom and the teacher asks a question that you know the answer to, but you don't raise your hand to answer for fear that you may be wrong? The little voice in your head says

"Don't answer because you might be wrong and if you're wrong then everyone else in the class will think you are stupid."

The voice believes it is to protecting you from harm. It's your inner self letting you know this is a strange and potentially harmful situation. Your subconscious mind can be helpful, but it can also be your detriment. It is there to keep you comfortable, to keep you safe. It will try to stop you from taking risks. Without risk there is no reward and without taking a risk and trusting yourself, you will never grow. Can you imagine how things would have turned out if the Wright brothers' didn't believe they were smart enough to fly a plane or if Christopher Columbus didn't dare to go against the status quo, and declare the earth was round instead of flat? We would all still be living in caves if we didn't dare to take risks. To grow we must believe in ourselves and take risks.

Ignore the little voice that is telling you, you are not smart enough to pursue an education. You are smart enough, because believe it or not it's not really about how smart you are that makes you successful. Smarts are only a small component. It is about how hard you are willing to work to accomplish your dreams. Even if you were not a good student in high school doesn't mean you will not be a good student in college. The two structures are entirely different. High school is too structured and robotic. You're day starts at 7:30 a.m. and ends at 3:00 pm. You go from English class to math class, to science class, to social studies until you have completed all of your classes for the day. What if you are not a morning person and you perform better in the afternoon? Unlike high school, the college structure is 100% designed by you. You can take classes in the afternoon, or in the evening, if that works best for you. You can pick the courses you like, and the professors that better suit you're learning style. You can choose one class a day or five a day. You can select classes that are hours apart from each other that give you time to go home and take a nap or study in between. It is entirely up to you. College is extremely flexible. If you don't have the time to be physically on campus you could select an online course and study from home.

Be creative and put yourself into a position to succeed. If the thought of going to college is still intimidating, try starting with just one class. Work hard and smart and you will discover you are smarter than you give yourself credit for. Once you have done that then the momentum starts to build and before you know it you will be walking up to the podium to accept your diploma.

CHAPTER 7
THE MOTIVATION

Now that we have gotten past the excuses of why we can't attend class, let's talk about what will keep us there. Anything and everything we want to achieve in our lives can be obtained. Our level of success is based upon our level of motivation. Some of the best motivation in the world that makes you focused and passionate about the situation at hand, is what I like to call **Pressure based motivation.** It's the motivation that moves us to react and act swiftly.

Merriam Webster dictionary defines pressure as: *The burden of physical or mental distress* or *the stress or urgency of matters demanding attention.*

Often times when we think of pressure, we think of it as being a negative. "I was pressured into making a decision." "The pressure of the roaring crowd caused the player to miss the game winning free throw." Pressure can indeed cause anxiety, but if used constructively, I believe pressure can be used positively because it jumps out and grabs you and forces you into action. It can help define what type of person you are. When the pressure of a situation is thrust upon you, you have no other opportunity but to react. Your goal becomes very clear and all outside forces that do not involve the situation at hand become irrelevant.

We have heard the story many times of a young child who went swimming alone at a local pond. This young child drifted out into the water too far and begins to struggle to stay afloat. The child fears for his life and screams out for help.

Now you are sitting on the water bank enjoying the nice summer day when you hear this child scream out for help. You don't know how to swim either, but you are the only one in the area who can help. What do you do? On a normal day you would never go into the water for fear of drowning, but now the pressure is on, you have to save this drowning child. Nothing else in the world matters except returning this child to safety, the pressure forces you into action. You don't care about your inability to swim, you react without a second thought. You jump into the water and manage to stay afloat long enough to bring the child back to dry land. You had no idea you were going to save someone life that day, however it was pressure that made you swim regardless of not knowing how to swim, and as a reward you becoming a hero that day.

Let's look at another scenario where pressure motivates you into action. Let's say your job tells you there is a free online training

course that the company offers that will take several hours of your personal time to complete. The training is optional, and not mandatory. However, they do guarantee the training will increase your knowledge of your position and make you a stronger and more attractive employee. If you have a busy life and have no time to take a free online course. You may ignore the free training and focus your time on maintaining your current lifestyle. In this scenario no pressure was applied at all and no true growth was gained.

Now, what if your job told you, you have 24 hours to complete a mandatory online training course that the company offers that will take several hours to complete. There is one stipulation; you will have to take an exam after this course that you must pass in order to keep your current position. If you fail the course you will lose your job. Now the pressure is on 100%. Taking and passing this online course becomes a top priority in your life. Things that seemed important now take a momentary backseat to this online course. You go home that day and ask the family to take care of dinner and you ask the children to make sure their homework is taken care of and you ask your oldest child to make sure they assist their younger sibling in taking their nightly shower and dressing for bed. Now you have time to focus on the online course. You cram for the course all evening and the next day you pass the exam with flying colors. You discover after taking the course your knowledge of the job has increased exponentially. You apply this knowledge to your current position and within one year you are promoted and receive a twenty five percent increase in salary and an extra week's vacation. This increase gives you the money and time to take a week's vacation with the family to Disneyland.

In both scenarios the goal was to increase your knowledge through a free online course. A momentary sacrifice and an increase in pressure allowed you the opportunity to better yourself and it also allowed your family the opportunity to step up their levels of responsibilities even if it was for only one evening.

Did the pressure help or hurt in this situation? I say it helped because it pressured you to better yourself.

Pressure can be your best friend and pressure can be your worst enemy. It is all based upon how you apply it to your life. Sometimes the pressure of a situation isn't there. We have to apply it to ourselves to make things happen. Even if the free online course wasn't mandatory, we should still treat it as if it is. We must force ourselves to be better, to constantly grow and become stronger candidates to all things in our lives.

Once we have convinced ourselves that an education is the next logical step in the process of reaching our goals and obtaining our dreams, we must apply the pressure to ourselves when it comes to obtaining this education. We have to treat the situation as if our life and livelihood depends upon it. We will not tell ourselves that we will wait for the time to be perfect. The time is now. Act upon it.

CHAPTER 8
THE POWER WITHIN TO ACCOMPLISH ANYTHING

The best way to begin your journey in achieving an education is to start with the end in mind. Imagine being in your dream job or starting your own dream business. Don't worry about how you're going to do it. Start and only concern yourself with the "WHAT." The "WHAT" is achieving an education, hearing your name called as you walk on stage to accept your diploma. Once you have focused your drive and attention on the "WHAT", the "HOW" will present itself. Take a moment and write down all of the things a quality education can give you and how it can improve your life.

Place this list near your bed so it is the first thing you see in the morning, or place it on your refrigerator or near the bathroom sink so you see it when you brush your teeth in the morning, and at night. Put it in a location that is very visible and works for you, but make sure you read the list every day and while you are reading it envision your new life. The thought will begin as just that, a thought of how your life can be. The more you focus; the thought will shift from your conscious mind to your subconscious. The subconscious mind is where the magic resides. The subconscious mind is what actually controls the way you feel and think.

Once the idea is burned into your subconscious the path to success will reveal itself. Now when you envision your future make sure you dream big. Don't settle on what you think you can accomplish, reach for more. Often times we underestimate our abilities and select the path that is the easiest to obtain. If you are unsure of your ability, it is ok to start with focusing on one class at a time, but in the back of your mind think bigger and better. If an Associate's degree is your goal envision a Bachelor's degree, if a Bachelor's degree is your goal envision a Master's degree and if a Master's degree is your goal envision obtaining a Doctorate.

Now is the time to take control of your life. That "one day" you have talked about for years, is today. Be great. You have it in you. We all have power inside of us to be spectacular. Remember to stay positive. Start with obtaining information on a specific major that you are interested in. You could attend a college information night that gives you all of the details of the major you are interested in or you could visit the website of the college and program you are interested in. You can also go the traditional yet very informative route, and contact the college or university you're interested in and make an appointment to see an advisor and they can help you map out your path to success and find out what program

works best for you and your lifestyle. After this is accomplished it is just

as simple as registering for your first class or classes and attending.

CHAPTER 9
BREAKING THE COMFORT ZONE

As we discussed in earlier chapters we all have our own personal level of comfort. There is nothing wrong with being comfortable. Why wouldn't we want to feel safe or have a life that is easy and stress free? When the clock alarm goes off on a cold Monday morning, the comfort of the bed feels awesome, especially on a snowy winter day. We would just love to stay under the warm covers all day and nap. If we could we would hide ourselves from the world, even if it were just for a few days or until at least the beginning of spring; however we know there is a world out there waiting for us to conquer. The world would just stop functioning if we all decided to never leave the comforts of our homes. So leaving our comfort zone is only temporary, however the effects can be positively tremendous. After leaving their morning beds we have surgeons saving or improving several lives throughout the day, an astronaut orbiting the earth, a scientist discovering a cure for a disease, a teacher teaching her class about American history or simply a student's first day of college. In all events it was the people's choice to leave their comfort zone and because of it they are rewarded with enriched lives. You have to leave your comfort zone to enrich your life. A quality education will open this pathway.

Let's take a moment and look at the Comfort Level Zone diagram below.

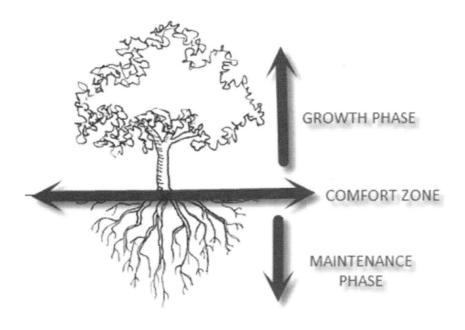

Like the diagram the phases of our lives are like the growth of a tree, and it is up to us to determine where we want to be in life.

The maintenance phase is where we set our roots in life. The comfort zone is where the tree breaks ground. It starts out small but has the potential to bud into an enormous fruitful tree. The final phase is the growth phase. This is where we break out beyond our comfort zones and start to branch out into new things in our lives that make us better and help us grow into a full blown tree.

THE MAINTENANCE PHASE

The maintenance phase is where we set our roots. It's the phase where we find soil and decide where we are going to plant the seed of our lives. For some of us the soil we choose may be rich and for others the soil may be not as fertile. It is entirely up to you to select the path of your life. Although this is a very important phase, we must remember this is only a starting point and in order for us to grow and reach our full potential we must not get stuck in this phase. There are plenty of us that get stuck in this phase and can spend our entire lives merely surviving, or barely staying afloat. In this phase we live paycheck to paycheck and in some cases the paycheck doesn't cover all of our bills or needs in our lives. In the maintenance phase if we miss one paycheck it could mean losing our car, or not being able to pay the rent. A missed paycheck could mean not being able to pay our utilities bills and having no electricity in our apartment. This phase is characterized with low paying dead end jobs, no retirement savings and basically no future. This is not the phase we want to settle our lives in.

COMFORT ZONE

The comfort zone can be classified as the American dream. This is the phase that we most aspire to be in. As the title describes, this is where we feel the most comfort. This is when we are able to have a mortgaged home and car loans. We can afford to have a nice wardrobe for ourselves and our family. We can shop on a budget and not worry about having enough money to pay our bills. If we choose, we can go out to dinner several times a week. We can afford to take vacations to our favorite locations. We may have to save money to pay for the trip or budget our expenses throughout the year, but a week or two away will not break the bank. If we have children we can afford to buy them all of the new fancy toys.

Our job may offer a 401k or a retirement program, and in this phase we may have enough saved salary to stay afloat for one month to three months without sinking underwater. Even though we may be comfortable in this phase there is a good chance that our current job is not a job we have a passion for. This can be a dangerous phase for our mental wellbeing, because if we are comfortable in our lives, our willingness to want to change and pursue something better becomes even more difficult. In this phase we feel we have a lot to risk or give up while pursuing our dreams. We are willing to work a job we don't really like for thirty years simply because it pays our bills and keeps us comfortable in our current lifestyle.

What would happen if we lost this comfortable job? Do we have the experience and education to find something that is of equal value or better?

Let go of the comfort and educate yourself. Make yourself more marketable, pursue your dreams. Live the life you want to live.

THE GROWTH PHASE

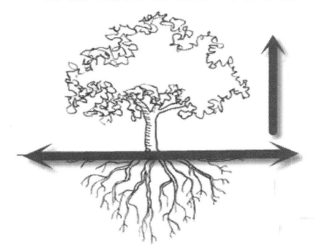

The growth phase is the most important phase of them all. In this phase you are stepping out of your current comfort zone and into true growth. The seed you planted in the maintenance phase has helped you blossom into a full-fledged beautiful tree with your branches fully extended out towards the sky and all of your dreams.

In this phase you are pushing your abilities to their full potential. You no longer call your occupation a job because in actuality it is your passion. You are no longer worried about waking up on a Monday morning to punch the clock. Instead you cannot wait to get up and get back to the job you love, because it has been running through your mind all weekend. In this phase you are financially and mentally stable. You no longer worry about having enough

money to pay your bills. You have fully maximized your retirement savings along with your own personal savings

In the growth phase you have truly become self-aware. You know who you are as a person. You fully understand your strengths and your weaknesses, and most importantly you know what you want out of life. In the growth phase you can be seriously working on your degree or have already finished your degree. In either case you will be able to feel a serious change in your life and your mental attitude. As you take yourself and your degree seriously, it will ooze from your pores and others will begin to take you serious as well. The growth phase is where you want to thrive to be in all aspects of your life. Every day you are working on making yourself better. You are no longer happy with just surviving or being a little comfortable. When you are in the growth phase you will not only be able to help yourself, but your focus will shift to helping others reach this level as well. Now you can pause for a moment and realize you are truly enjoying life.

Pursuing an education is the way to break through your comfort zone and push your way to the growth phase, where you love and live life based upon your passions.

CHAPTER 10
THE FIRST BRICK

Ok so we have read through the book and hopefully we learned some very valuable lessons about ourselves and about how we can improve our lives. We have set aside any excuses that will hinder our pursuits of an education. We respect the excuses that may stop us from pushing forward, but we understand that they are just that, Excuses, nothing more nothing less. We understand that having to find the time to go to class, can be a challenge, but there is indeed a time for everything in our lives, we have to sit down and prioritize and make small sacrifices to accomplish our goals. We understand that getting a quality education is not free and there are so many options out there that can help us finance our education and our dreams. We understand that investing in ourselves should be our top priority.

Have you ever flown in a commercial airplane? If you have you will know right before takeoff the stewardess goes through the safety precautions in case of an emergency. One of the first things she says is if the airplane loses cabin pressure an oxygen mask will deploy from the compartment above your head to be used to help you breath. She informs you that if you are traveling with small children make sure you secure your mask first before helping them.

It may sound funny, but this stewardess just gave you one of the keys to life. Help yourself first to get better and be secure and when you do that you will have the ability to help others be safe and secure. I smile every time I fly in an airplane and hear the steward or stewardess say this because as basic as it sounds, it so, so true.

Hopefully this book also helps us to understand we all have obligations and needs to attend to in life and sometimes we have to carve a little space in these needs for our own personal growth, and if we have children or obligations that make juggling the task of going to class and managing life difficult, an education will not hinder, but enhance your life. We also understand that we all have the smarts to be successful in school, we have to be creative and most important we have to be able to know it is our efforts that get us to the stage in front of the large audience of family and friends as we stand tall and accept our diploma.

We will take the pressure and use it as our motivation to push forward. Sometimes the pressure will not be there so we have to apply it ourselves to grow. We will not be afraid of the pressure, instead we will embrace it and us it as a vehicle that drives us towards our goals of getting a degree. We understand that comfort can be our enemy that comfort can keep us stagnant with no growth. We will operate above what makes us comfortable and get out and experience life, take classes and meet new people. This will help us develop a network that can springboard us to levels of success we never thought we could achieve. At the end of the day we know we have the power to achieve anything we set our mind to. Once we believe, we know that we can achieve. We know we have to sit down and determine where we want to be in life. What do we want to do? What are our passions?

After we determine what we are passionate about we must find out what place of higher learning can get us there.

SO WHAT IS THE FIRST STEP?

The first step is like laying down the first brick in our wall of success. We won't worry about the entire wall we will just focus on putting down the first brick.

The first step is registering for your first class and smiling the smile of success when you attend your first class. Before you walk into the class for the first time, take a deep breath and think about how this will be the first door you walkthrough to your future.

Good luck and I will see you at the finish line.

Made in the USA
San Bernardino, CA
27 August 2018